8/6

Günter Gerngross • Herbert Puchta

PLAYWAY 2
TO ENGLISH

Pupil's Book

IN COLLABORATION WITH
ANGELA HORAK • GUDRUN ZEBISCH

Illustrations by Svjetlan Junaković

ISBN 0521 656834

Layout by Gio Festin

© Cambridge University Press and Helbling, Rum/Innsbruck • Esslingen 1998

First published 1998

Fifth printing 2005

CAMBRIDGE
UNIVERSITY PRESS

Helbling

1, 2, 3,
4, 5, 6, 7,
8, 9, 10,

CLOWN
CORNFLAKES PUZZLE

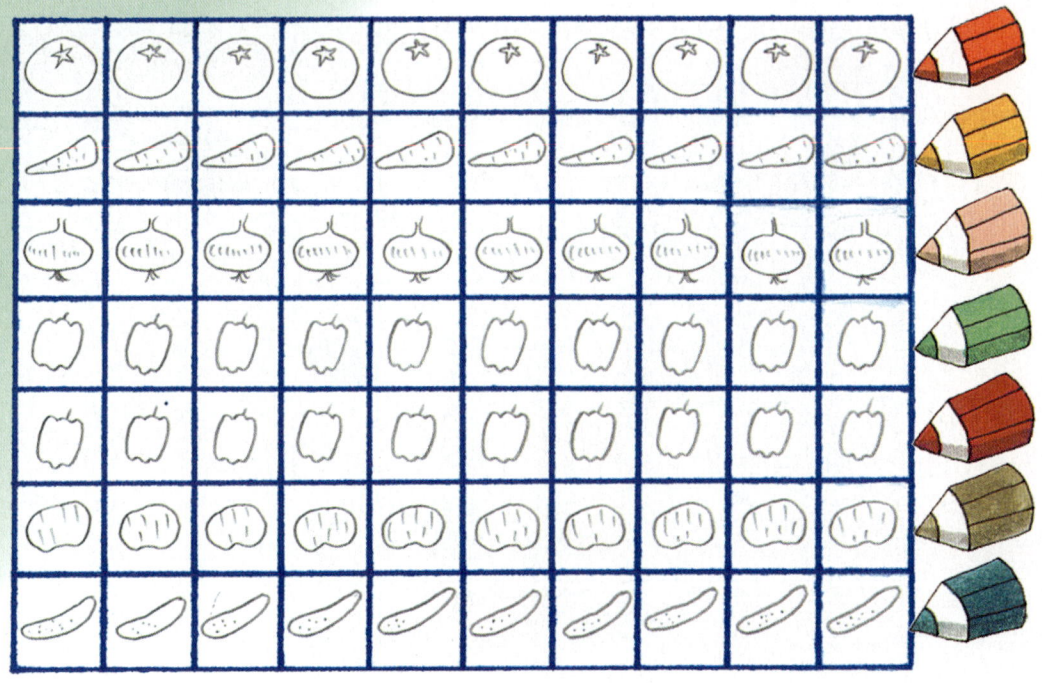

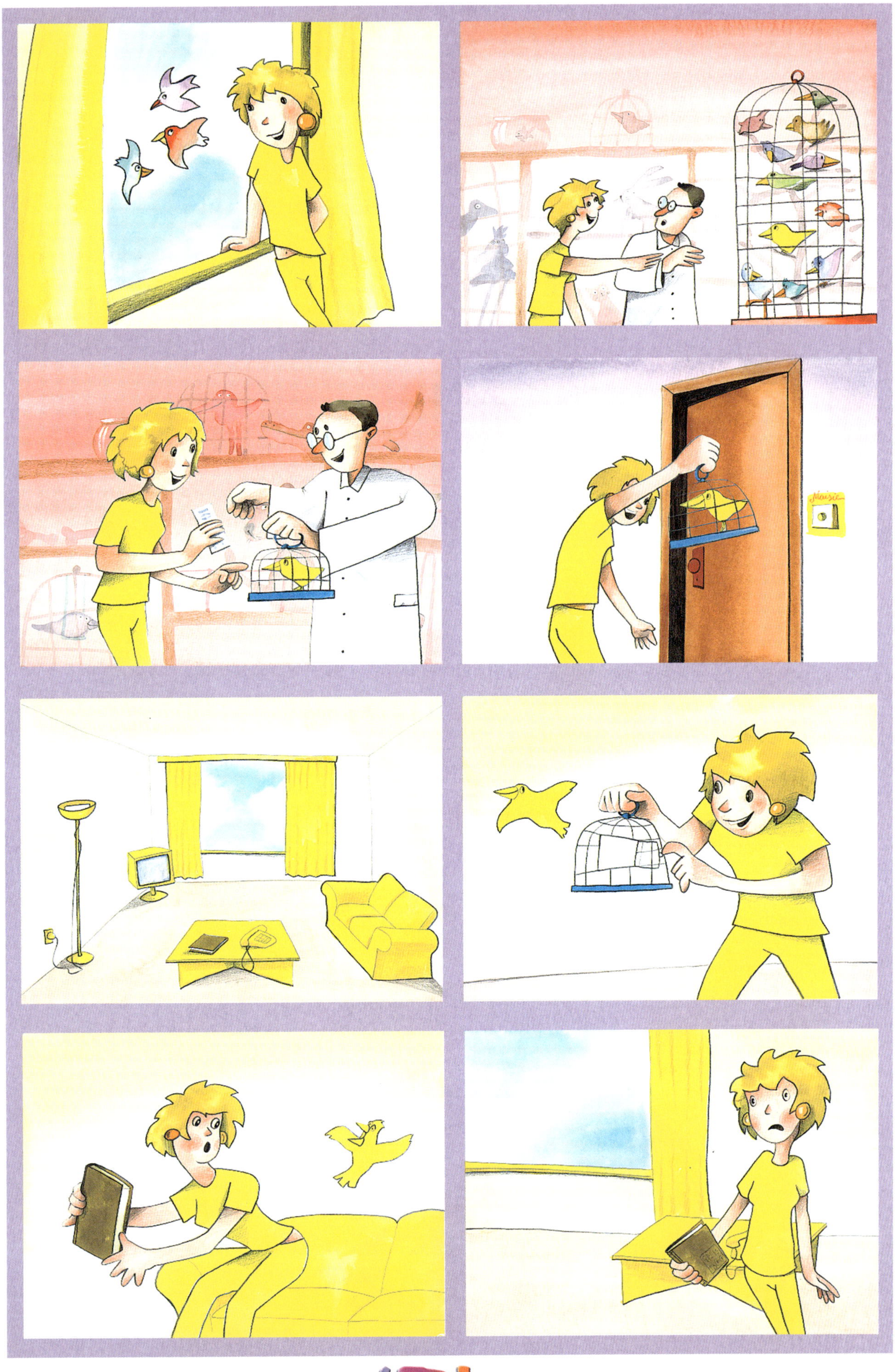

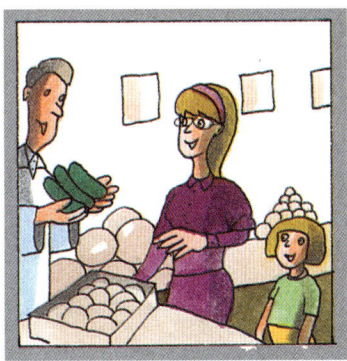

1.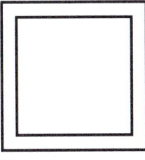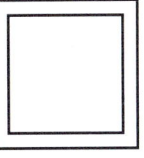

2.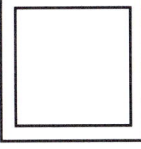

3.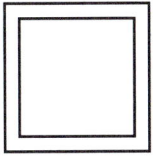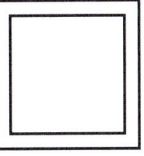

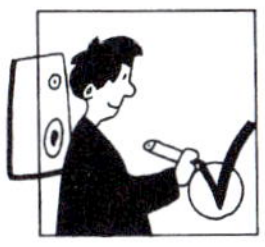

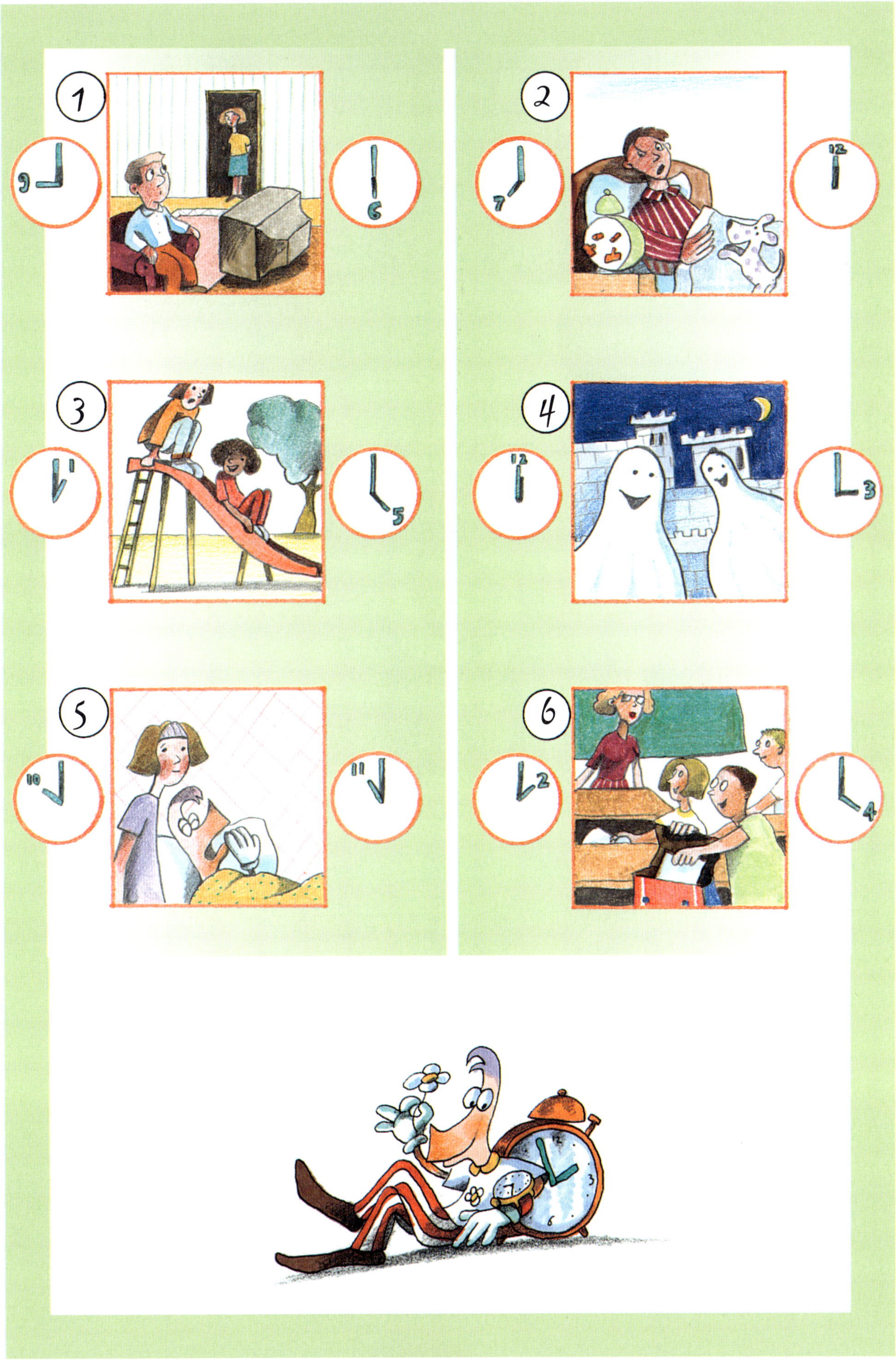
1
2
3
4
5
6

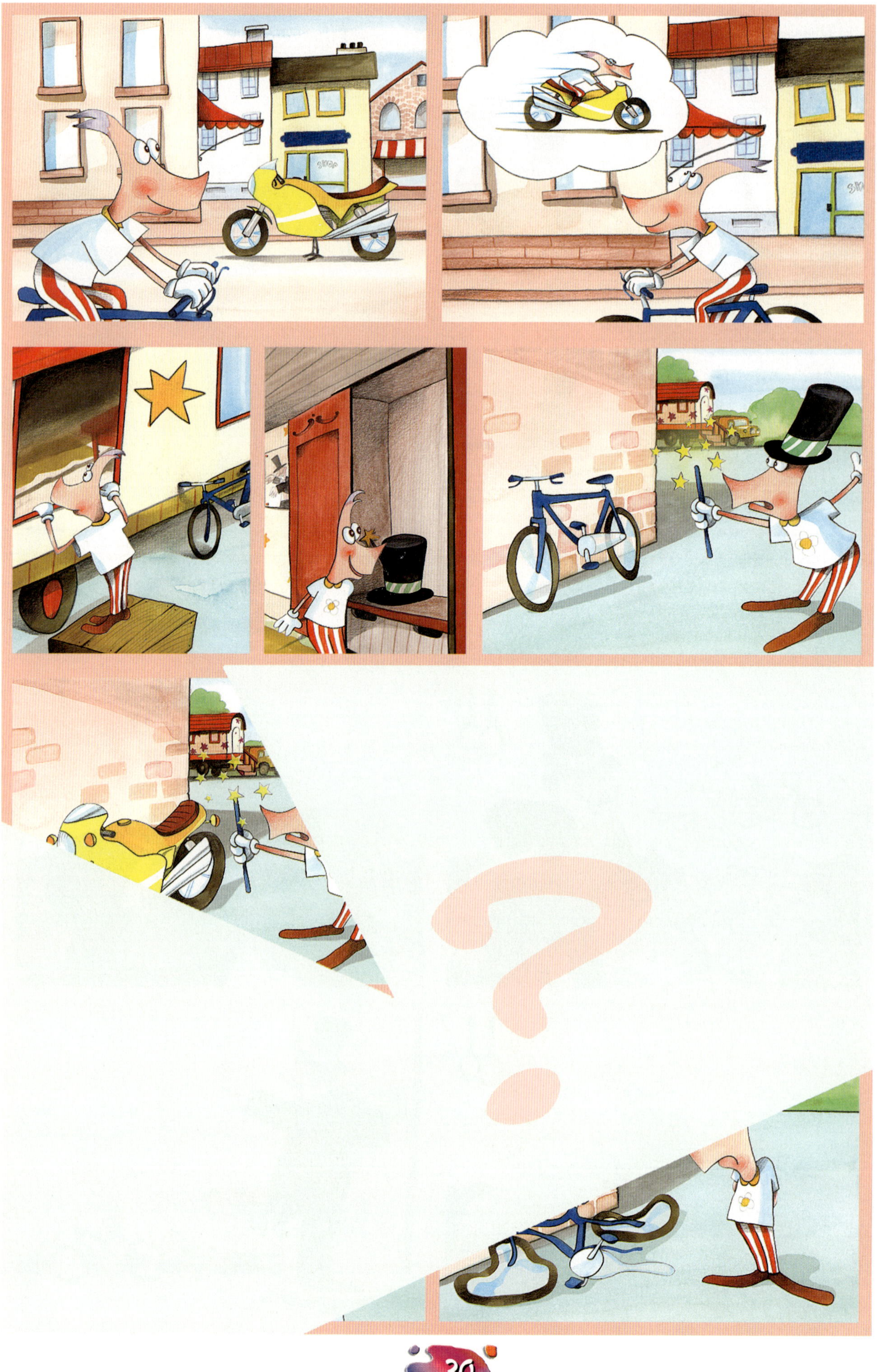

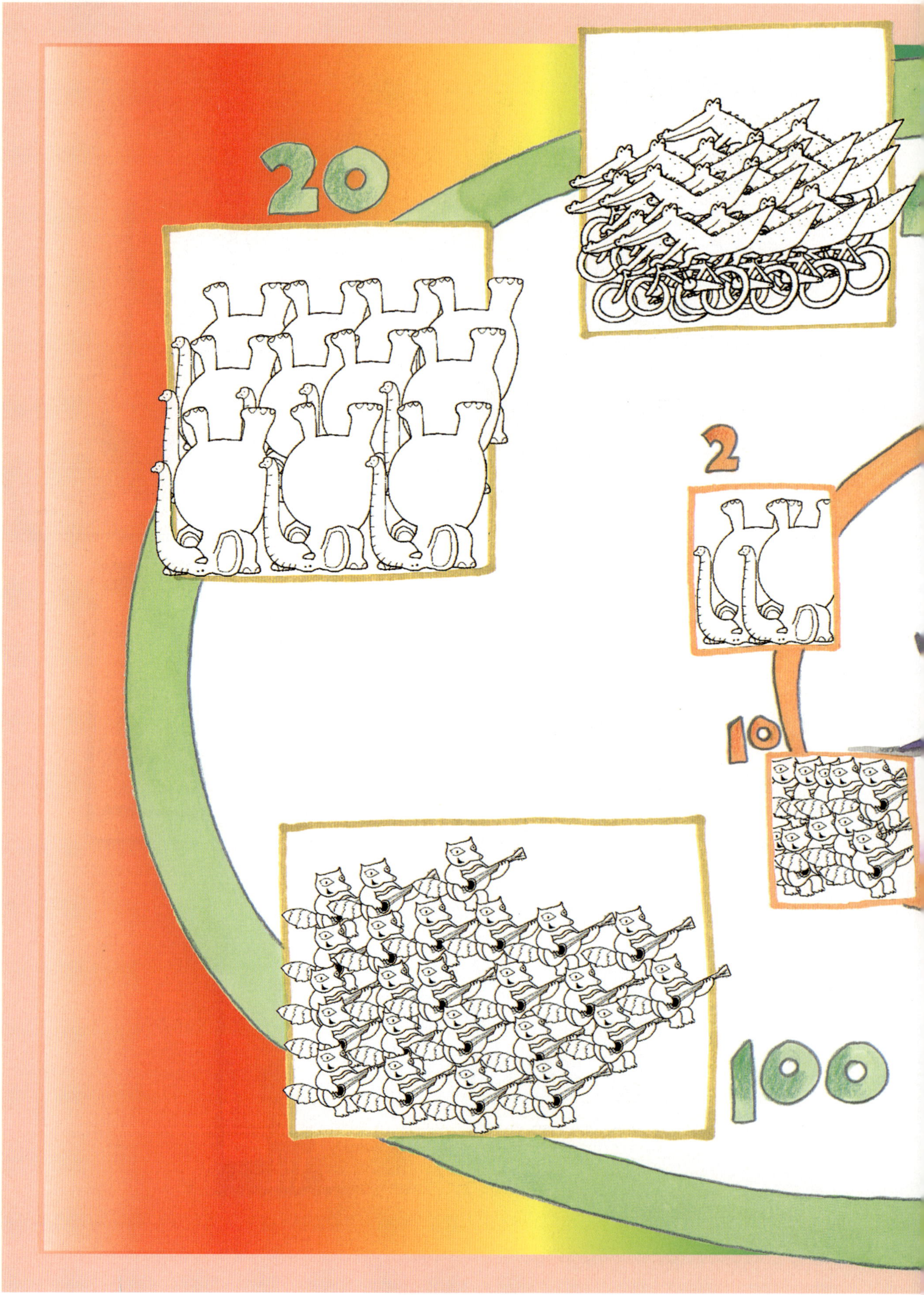

20

2

10

100

60

4

6

8

80

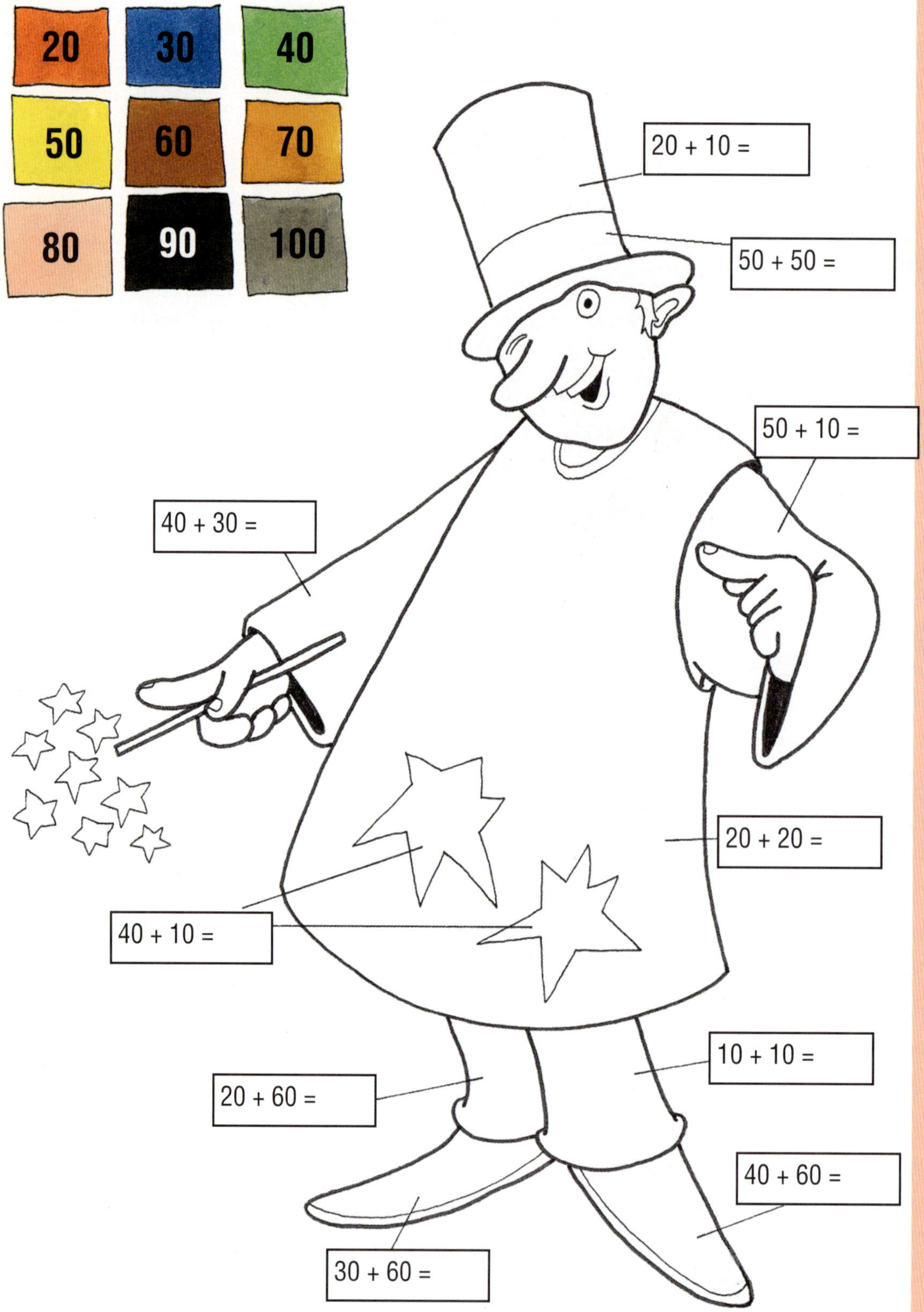

20	**30**	**40**
50	**60**	**70**
80	**90**	**100**

20 + 10 =

50 + 50 =

50 + 10 =

40 + 30 =

20 + 20 =

40 + 10 =

10 + 10 =

20 + 60 =

40 + 60 =

30 + 60 =

1.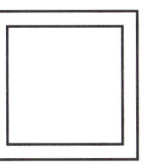

2.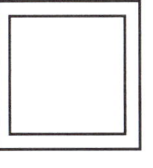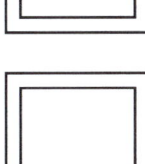

3.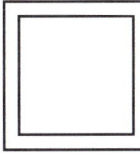

START

FINISH

STOP

STOP

STOP

1.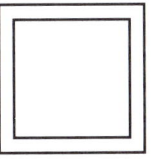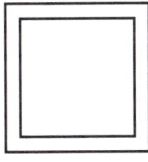

2.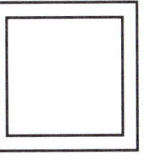

3.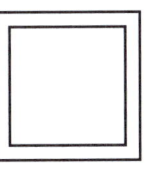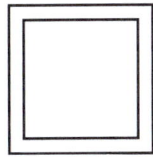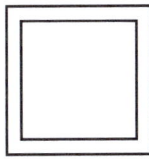

EDDIE   FRED

ROCKIE   RONNIE

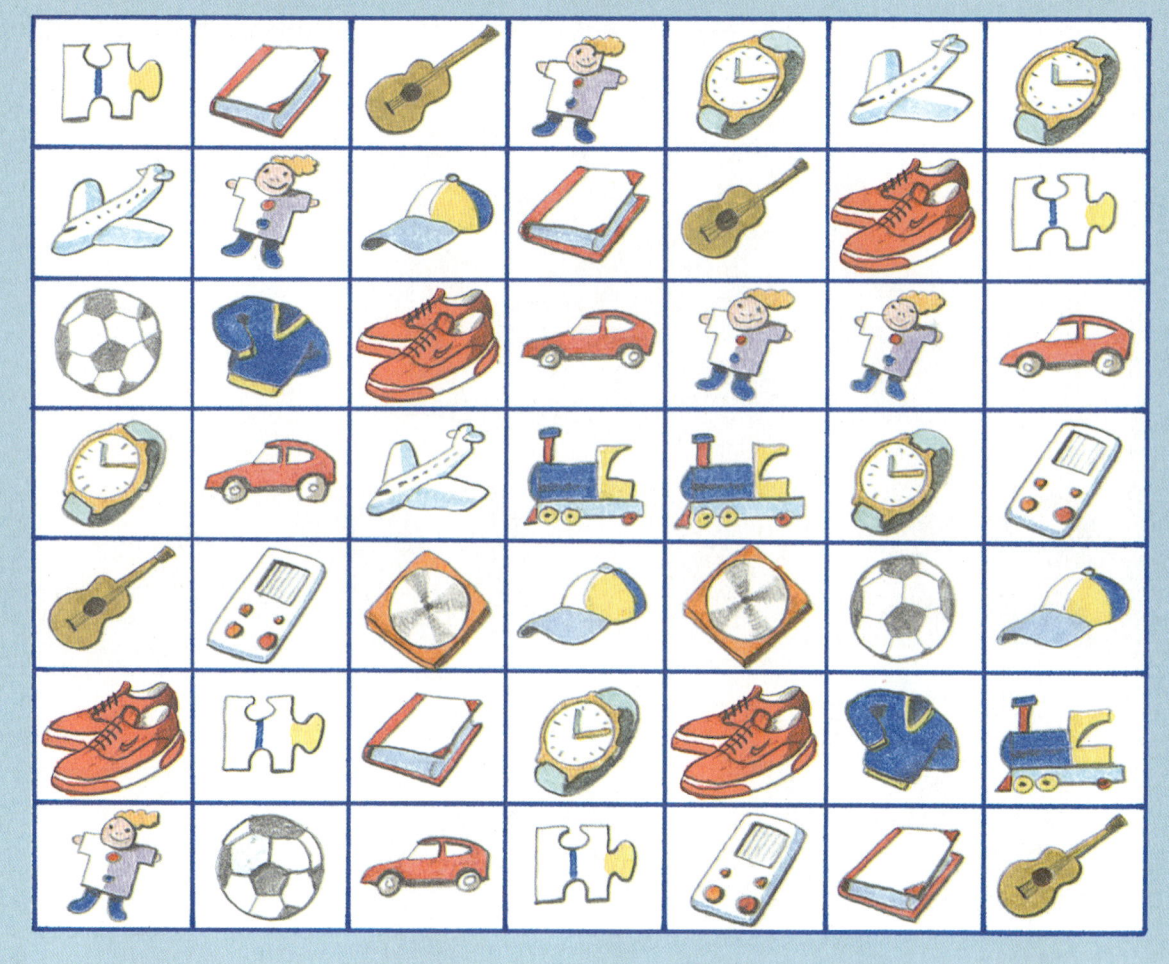

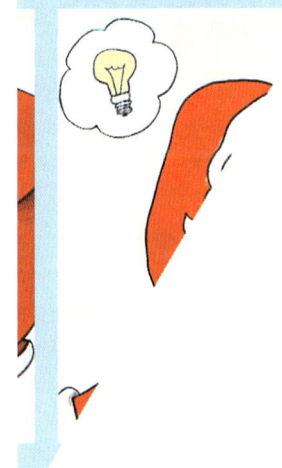

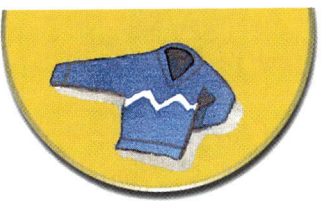